by Alexa Ludeman & Emily Wessel

Tin Can Knits

Vancouver, CANADA

To get your complimentary electronic copy of this book, visit www.tincanknits.com/ebook

contents

Published by Tin Can Knits 2011

www.tincanknits.com
ISBN 978-0-9877628-0-1

Layout by Emily Wessel
Second Edition 2014
Printed and bound in the UK and the USA

1
2
3
4
5
6
7
8
9

other Tin Can Knits books :::

tin can knits :::

seamless knits with a signature mix of retro quirkiness and playful attitude

Alexa is a talented photographer who is very passionate about knitting and design. She is mother to our lovely model Hunter, the inspiration for this collection.

Emily is crazy about knit design, in love with lace. Her eye for unique and sensible construction combined with her wild creativity make her designs a clear hit! Emily's adventurous spirit has taken her across the pond to Edinburgh, UK, but in her heart she is a Vancouver Island girl.

At Tin Can Knits we create irresistible knits and offer outstanding pattern support. Check out our **website** and **blog** for in-depth tutorials covering techniques from knit and purl to advanced lace design. Get in touch to let us know what you think: **tincanknits@gmail.com**

connect online :::      

introductions

Alexa Ludeman + Emily Wessel = Tin Can Knits

From striking lace and cables, to comforting knit and purl, 9 Months of Knitting has patterns for knitters of every level.

Baby leg-warmers, a cute cardigan, two blankets and a hand-knitted undersea garden: 9 Months is full of patterns with a refreshing blend of retro quirkiness and playful attitude.

This first collection from Tin Can Knits includes nine patterns for babies, toddlers, and their parents, all knit in machine washable wools for ease of care.

Cast on and enjoy the knits!

how-tos

abbreviations, techniques, and helpful suggestions

using this book: *Please enjoy responsibly.* This book is intended as a pattern collection rather than an instructional tome; consult the internet or a knitting reference book for techniques not covered here.

gauge and sizing: You knew you should knit a swatch, but you didn't, and the baby sweater is too small. We must refer you to Elizabeth Zimmerman, who famously noted that babies come in all sizes; find the baby that fits! Gauge in this book is measured over stockinette stitch, after blocking. Our patterns have sizes noted by age, but it is most useful to refer to the finished measurements when choosing your size. When in doubt, knit the next largest size.

pattern adjustments: Some of our patterns include hints and information on how to adjust the size. Keep in mind that adjusting the size will affect the amount of yarn required.

yarn substitutions: This collection is designed predominantly in machine-washable yarns, for new Moms' sanity. When substituting, consider fibre content, drape, stretch, and stitch definition, as well as gauge.

charts: Each chart square represents a stitch as indicated by the key. Repeats are indicated by heavy lines, and are worked as many times as will fit in each round or row. As you will notice, some charts illustrate every row (or round), and others illustrate only RS or odd numbered rows (or rounds), with the WS or even numbered rows or rounds described by text instructions. Always refer to chart notes and key before you begin.

techniques: Advanced techniques used in our patterns are briefly described here. For techniques not covered, see **www.tincanknits.com**

crochet chain provisional cast on: With waste yarn make a slip knot. Insert crochet hook, yarn over, pull through a loop. Continue to yarn over and pull loops through the previous loop until you have a crochet chain of a few more stitches than you plan to cast on. Now with knitting needles and working yarn, insert needle under back bump of last crochet chain stitch. Yarn over and pull up a stitch. Continue along crochet chain, creating as many sts as required for cast on. When the time comes to 'unpick' the provisional cast on, unfasten the end, and it should 'unzip', leaving live stitches to be worked.

i-cord: Cast on 3 (or more) stitches on a DPN. Knit 1 row. [Move all stitches to other end of needle, pull yarn tight across back of stitches, and knit another row] repeat until i-cord is desired length, then draw yarn tail through remaining live stitches and secure.

i-cord cast on: Cast on 3 stitches. Knit into front and back of first stitch (kfb), knit 2. You now have 4 stitches on the RH needle. Do not turn your work. [Slip 3 stitches back to the LH needle. Knit into front and back of first stitch, knit 2] repeat until you have cast on the desired number of stitches + 2. Turn work. Bind off 1 stitch purlwise. Slip stitch back to LH needle. Purl 2 together. Slip stitch back to LH needle. Proceed following pattern. If knitting in the round, there will be a gap between the two ends of the i-cord edge. Sew up this gap using the yarn tail to create a continuous edge.

picking up stitches:

Along an edge: With RS facing, insert needle between stitches (or rows), yarn over with working yarn on WS, and pull a loop through knitted fabric to RS (*one st picked up*). Repeat until desired number of sts have been picked up.

From RS of work where WS is inaccessible: With RS facing, insert needle between sts (or rows), and back to RS of work, yarn over with working yarn on RS, and use needle to pull a loop through knitted fabric back to RS (*one st picked up*). Repeat until desired number of sts have been picked up. You may find this technique easier to accomplish with a crochet hook.

pinhole cast on: To begin, create a circle using the end of the yarn. Pinch the circle in your left hand, and hold the needle and working yarn in your right hand. You will create new stitches using the point of the needle, working into the centre of the circle *(some knitters find using a crochet hook is easier).*

1. Insert needle into circle from front to back
2. Wrap yarn around needle
3. Use needle point to bring loop through circle from back to front (1 new loop on needle)
4. Wrap working yarn around needle point (2 new loops on needle)
5. Use finger to lift first loop over second loop and off the needle (1 loop remains, this is one stitch cast on)

Repeat steps 1-5 until you have cast on the desired number of stitches. Pull on the yarn end to close the circle up to a tiny spot in the centre of the work.

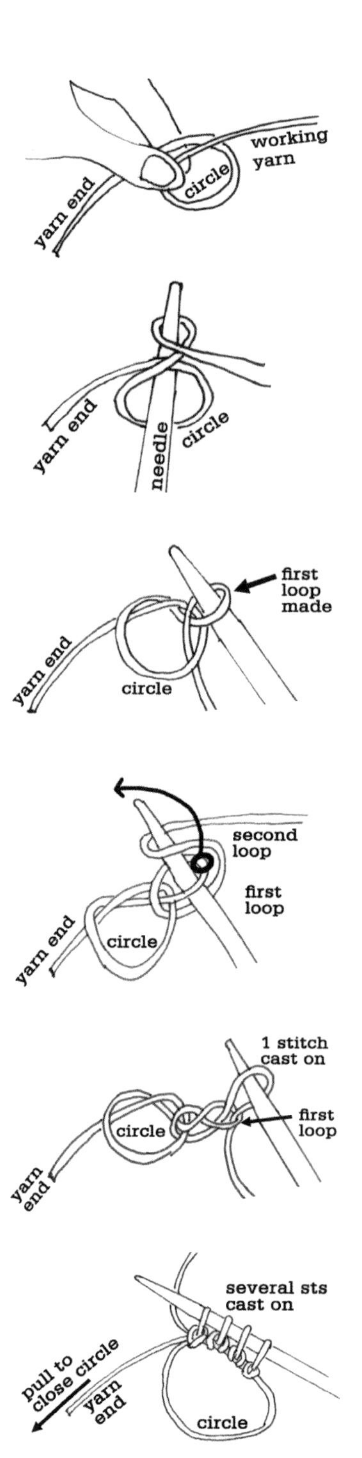

short row shaping: To work short rows, you knit part of the way through a row or round, but turn around before you get to the end, and begin working in the opposite direction, on the other side of the work. Work as pattern specifies to the point where the pattern says 'wrap and turn'. To 'wrap and turn', you will knit the last stitch indicated, then bring yarn to the front of the work, slip the next st purlwise from LH needle to RH needle, pass yarn back to back of work. Then turn work so opposite side is facing you, and slip the stitch back from what is now the LH needle back to the RH needle (without working it). The yarn will now 'wrap' around the base of this unworked stitch. Continue to work per the pattern. When the pattern says 'pick up wraps and knit them together with the stitches they wrap', this means that when you come to a wrapped stitch, slip it to the RH needle, then pick up the wrap on the LH needle, then slip the stitch back to the LH needle, and knit the wrap and the stitch together (using either a k2tog or p2tog, as makes sense to maintain the stitch pattern).

stretchy bind-off: K1, [k1, place both sts back on LH needle, and k2tog-tbl] repeat to end. Cut yarn and pull through final stitch.

abbreviations: find the full list at **www.tincanknits.com**

c2b, c4b, c6b	**cable 2 (4, 6) back** - slip 1 (2, 3) sts to cn, hold in back of work, knit 1 (2, 3) sts from LH needle, knit 1 (2, 3) sts from cn
c2f, c4f, c6f	**cable 2 (4, 6) front** - slip 1 (2, 3) sts to cn, hold in front of work, knit 1 (2, 3) sts from LH needle, knit 1 (2, 3) sts from cn
CC	contrast colour
CO	cast on
cn	cable needle
dec	decrease(d)
DPNs	double pointed needles
inc	increase(d)
k	knit
k2tog	knit two stitches together
k3tog	knit three stitches together
kfb	knit into the front and back of the same stitch
LH	left hand
m1	make one stitch (by preferred method)
m1L	make one left - use LH needle to lift bar between sts from front, knit into back of loop
m1R	make one right - use LH needle to lift bar between sts from back, knit into front of loop
MC	main colour
N1(2,3)	needle 1(2,3)
p	purl
p2tog	purl two stitches together
p3tog	purl three stitches together
PM	place marker
rep	repeat
RH	right hand
rnd(s)	round(s)
RS	right side of the work
sl1	slip one stitch (purlwise unless otherwise specified)
sl1-k2tog-psso	slip 1 knitwise, knit two together, pass slipped stitch over
ssk	slip 1 knitwise, slip 1 knitwise, knit 2 slipped sts together tbl
st.st.	stockinette stitch
st(s)	stitch(es)
tbl	through back loop(s) of stitch(es) (for example k1-tbl, or k2tog-tbl)
work as established	continue in pattern; knit the knit sts and purl the purl sts.
WS	wrong side of the work
w&t	short row wrap and turn
yds	yards
yo	yarn over

i heart rainbows

classic cutsie-pie fair-isle ❤ *by Emily Wessel and Alexa Ludeman*

Babies should be dressed in garments so sweet that they hurt your teeth just to look at. This joyfully saccharine little pullover tastes of Sweet Tarts, Rocket Pops and edible candy necklaces. OK ... I admit it, I watched the Care Bears as a child. Over and over and over again!

sizing:

Sweater: Premie (0-6 mo, 6-12 mo, 1-2 yrs, 2-4 yrs)
Finished chest measurement: 17 (20, 21.5, 23, 25) inches
Sleeve length from underarm: 5.5 (6.5, 7.5, 8.5, 10.5) inches
Length underarm to hem: 5.5 (6, 6.5, 8, 8) inches

Hat: baby (toddler, child, adult)
fits head circumference: 14 (16, 19, 21) inches

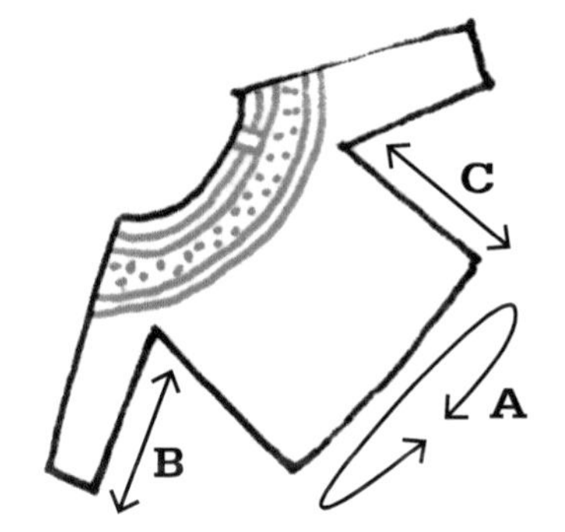

A - chest / bust
B - sleeve
C - underarm to hem

materials:

Yarn: Sock / fingering weight yarn

Pullover: Main colour (body): 300 (350, 400, 500, 600) yds
Contrast colours 1-6: 30 (40, 50, 60, 75) yds each colour

Hat: Main colour: 90 (100, 120, 150) yds
Contrast colours 1-6: 10 (15, 20, 25) yds

*(we used **SweetGeorgia Superwash Sock** in 'riptide', **SweetGeorgia Cashluxe Fine** in 'saffron', and **Koigu KPPM** in colours 1175, 2220, 1521, 1050, 1051)*

Needles: US #2 / 2.75mm and US #3 / 3.25 mm *(or as req'd to meet gauge);* 16" circular needle and DPNs in each size

Gauge: 28 sts / 4" in stockinette stitch *(on smaller needles)*

Notions: 3 little buttons, darning needle, waste yarn

i heart rainbows sweater: This pullover is knit from the top down. To begin, the collar and placket portion is knit back and forth, then the work is joined in the round for the fair-isle yoke, after which the work is split into body and arms and knit in the round to hem and cuffs.

yoke:

On smaller needles with MC, cast on 70 (78, 84, 88, 96) sts.
Knit 6 (6, 8, 8, 10) rows.

Increase row 1 (RS): k2, [m1, k2] to last 6 sts, k2, yo, k2tog, k2
[101 (113, 122, 128, 140) sts]
Row 2 (WS): k4, purl to last 4 sts, k4.

Knit 2-row rainbow stripes as follows:

Holding MC and CC1 together k4, drop MC, knit to end. Repeat row 2.
Holding CC1 and CC2 together k4, drop CC1, knit to end. Repeat row 2.
Holding CC2 and CC3 together k4, drop CC2, knit to last 4 sts, yo, k2tog, k2.
Repeat row 2.
Holding CC3 and CC4 together k4, drop CC3, knit to end. Repeat row 2.
Holding CC4 and CC5 together k4, drop CC4, knit to end. Repeat row 2.
Holding CC5 and CC6 together k4, drop CC5, knit to last 4 sts, yo, k2tog, k2.
Repeat row 2.
Holding CC6 and MC together k4, drop CC6, knit to end. Repeat row 2.

Increase and joining round (RS): knit 3 (3, 4, 4, 4), [m1, k2] to last 4 sts. Transfer last 4 sts from RH of circular needle onto a separate needle, hold in front of first 4 sts on LH needle and knit through 1 stitch on front needle and 1 stitch on back needle at the same time, knitting them together. Do the same for the remaining 3 sts. This joins the work together for knitting in the round and creates an overlap for the placket. Place marker to indicate start of round. The buttonholes will be on the outside portion of the placket.
[144 (162, 175, 184, 202) sts)

Knit 1 round in MC, increasing 6 (8, 5, 6, 8) sts evenly spaced.
[150 (170, 180, 190, 210) sts]

Switch to larger needles and work fair-isle pattern as shown on chart A for 10 rounds. Switch back to smaller needles, and work 2 rounds even in MC.

Increase round: *(follow instructions for your size)*

Premie:	k3, [m1, k3, m1, k4] to end	[192 sts]
0-6 mo:	k2, [m1, k3] to end	[226 sts]
6-12 mo:	[m1, k2, m1, k3] to end	[252 sts]
1-2 yrs:	[m1, k2, m1, k3, m1, k3] to last 6 sts, m1, k2, m1, k2, m1, k2	[262 sts]
3-4 yrs:	[m1, k3] to end	[280 sts]

All sizes: Knit 1 round in MC. Then knit 2-round stripes in contrast colours 6, 5, 4, 3, 2, and 1. Switch back to MC, and work 1 round. On next round, increase 2 (6, 0, 0, 8) sts, evenly spaced [194 (232, 252, 262, 288) sts]. Work 1 (2, 6, 8, 12) more rounds.

separate sleeves and body:

Place 40 (48, 52, 54, 60) sts on hold *(left sleeve)*, cast on 6 (6, 6, 8, 8) sts using backward loop cast-on *(left underarm)*, knit 57 (68, 74, 77, 84) sts *(back)*, place next 40 (48, 52, 54, 60) sts on hold *(right sleeve)*, cast on 6 (6, 6, 8, 8) sts using backward loop cast-on *(right underarm)*, knit 57 (68, 74, 77, 84) sts *(front)*. [126 (148, 160, 170, 184) sts]

Place marker and join for working in the round. Knit all rounds until work measures 5 (5.5, 6, 7.5, 7.5) inches from underarm *(or 0.5 inches short of desired length)*.

Work in garter stitch *(purl 1 round, knit 1 round)* for 0.5 inches. Bind off loosely.

chart A: work rounds 1-10

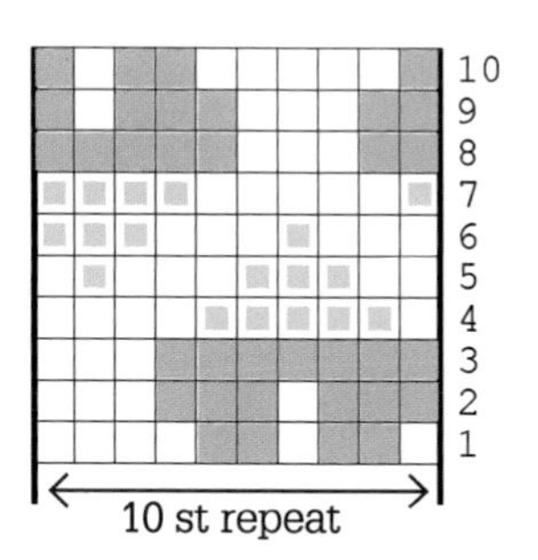

chart B: work rounds 1-6

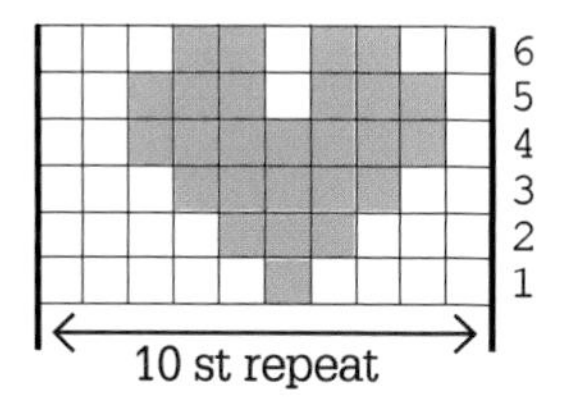

key and abbreviations

- ☐ MC - knit with main colour
- ■ CC1 - knit with contrast colour 1
- ▫ CC2 - knit with contrast colour 2

sleeves: *(work each the same)*

Place 40 (48, 52, 54, 60) held sts back on smaller size double pointed needles. Using MC pick up and knit 3 (3, 3, 4, 4) sts from the body, place marker to indicate underarm, then pick up and knit another 3 (3, 3, 4, 4) sts. Continue knitting around the sts on hold and picked up sts to underarm marker, which is the beginning of round from this point on. [46 (54, 58, 62, 68) sts]

Knit 5 rounds.
Work decrease round: k1, ssk, knit to last 3 sts, k2tog, k1. [2 sts dec]

Work decrease round every 6th round 3 (3, 4, 5, 6) more times.
[38 (46, 48, 50, 54) sts]

Work even until sleeve measures 5 (6, 7, 8, 10) inches from underarm *(or 0.5 inches short of total desired length).* Work in garter stitch *(purl 1 round, knit 1 round)* for 0.5 inches. Bind off loosely.

finishing: Weave in ends, sew on buttons at placket, block *(add white vinegar to wash water to prevent colours from running)*, and find an adorable cutie to dress up!

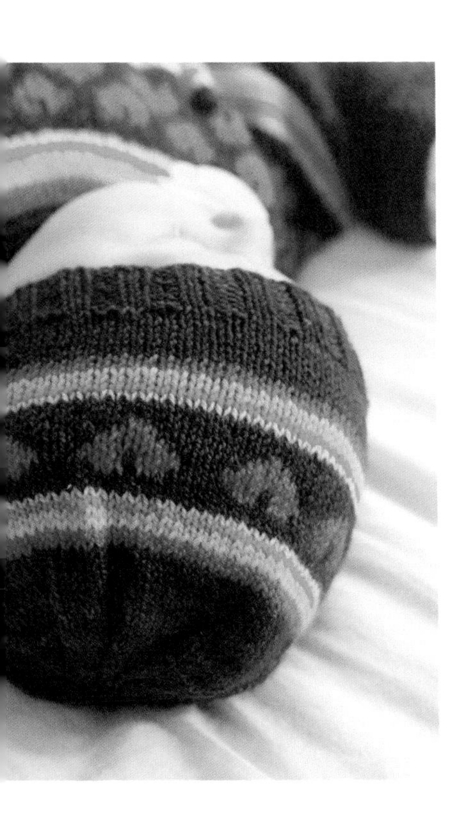

i heart rainbows hat:

Using MC and smaller needles cast on 88 (108, 120, 140) sts. Place marker and join for working in the round.

Ribbing: [k2, p2] around
Work as established in ribbing for 1 (1, 1.25, 1.5) inches.

Switch to larger needles and knit 1 round, increasing 2 (2, 0, 0) sts, evenly spaced. [90 (110, 120, 140) sts]. Knit 2 more rounds in MC. Then knit 1 (1, 1, 2) round(s) in each of the contrast colours 1, 2, 3, 4, 5, and 6. Knit 2 (2, 2, 3) rounds in MC.

Baby and toddler sizes: work rounds 1-6 of chart B
Child and adult sizes: work rounds 1-10 of chart A

Knit 2 (2, 2, 3) rounds in MC. Knit 1 (1, 1, 2) round(s) in each of the contrast colours 6, 5, 4, 3, 2, and 1 *(knit the rainbow in the reverse order to the first time that you knit it).*

Measure work, and if required, knit a few more rounds in MC until work measures 4 (5, 5.5, 6) inches from cast on. Setup for crown decreases as follows: [knit 9 (11, 12, 14) sts, place marker] around. You now have markers dividing the total sts into 10 equal sections.

Round 1: [knit to 2 sts before marker, k2tog] around [10 sts dec]
Round 2: knit

Work rounds 1-2 until 40 sts remain *(4 sts in each section).* Then work round 1 two more times [20 sts].

Next round: [k2tog] around [10 sts]

finishing: Break yarn, leaving a 6" tail. Thread tail through remaining stitches and pull tight to close. Weave in all ends, wet block the hat to adjust size and even out fair-isle pattern, and enjoy!

lumberjack

snuggly family fun in classic colours ❤ *by Alexa Ludeman*

These socks remind me of Dad, coming home from work as a heavy-duty mechanic out in logging camps. His big baby-blue Ford pickup rumbled up the driveway, and my mom, my sister and I ran outside, so excited to welcome him home.

sizing:

To Fit: Baby (Toddler, Child, **Mama, Papa**)

Baby: Cuff 5" (stretched) around, 2.5" long. Foot 3.5" long.
Toddler: Cuff 6.5" (stretched) around, 4.5" long. Foot 4.5" long.
Child: Cuff 7.5" (stretched) around, 5.5" long. Foot 6" long.
Mama: Cuff 10.5" (stretched) around, 6.25" long. Foot adjustable.
Papa: Cuff 13.5" (stretched) around, 7.5" long. Foot adjustable.

To adjust cuff or foot length simply knit shorter or longer in that section.

materials:

Yarn: DK weight yarn in 2 colours
Main Colour (MC): 75 (150, 200, **225, 350**) yds
Contrast Colour (CC): 25 (40, 50, **60, 75**) yds
*(we used **Madelinetosh Tosh DK** in 'silver fox' and 'tart')*

Needles: US #2 / 2.75mm and US #3 / 3.25mm *(or as req'd to meet gauge);* double pointed needles

Gauge: 24 sts / 4" in stockinette stitch *(on larger needles)*

pattern:

cuff: Using smaller needles and MC cast on 28 (36, 44, **52, 60**) sts and join for working in the round. The leg is worked entirely in ribbing: [k2, p2] around. Work a total of 5 (6, 6, **7, 9**) rounds in MC.

Switch to larger needles and work 1 round in MC. Switch to CC and work 2 (3, 3, **4, 6**) rounds. Switch to MC and work 1 (2, 2, **2, 4**) rounds. Switch to CC and work 2 (3, 3, **4, 6**) rounds. Switch to MC and work 10 (21, 28, **30, 32**) rounds *(or to desired cuff length).*

heel flap: Continue in MC. The heel flap is worked back and forth in rows.

Row 1 (RS): [k2, p2] three (4, 5, **6, 7**) times, k2, turn work *(you will be working with these 14 (18, 22, **26, 30**) sts for the heel; the remaining sts are on hold for the instep)*
Row 2 (WS): sl1, purl across, turn work
Row 3 (RS): [sl1, k1] across, turn work
Repeat rows 2-3 one (2, 2, **3, 5**) more time(s), then change to CC. Repeat rows 2-3 three (4, 4, **5, 7**) more times, then row 2 once more.

heel turn: Continue in CC.

Row 1 (RS): sl1, k7 (9, 11, **13, 15**), ssk, k1, turn
Row 2 (WS): sl1, p3, p2tog, p1, turn
Row 3: sl1, k4, ssk, k1, turn
Row 4: sl1, p5, p2tog, p1, turn

Baby Sock only:
Row 5 (RS): sl1, k6, ssk, turn
Row 6 (WS): sl1, p6, p2tog, turn
Row 7: knit across the 8 heel sts left

For Toddler, Child, Mama, and Papa Socks:
Row 5 (RS): sl1, knit to 1 st before the gap, ssk, k1, turn
Row 6 (WS): sl1, purl to 1 st before the gap, p2tog, p1, turn
Repeat rows 5-6 until 1 st remains on each end.

Next row (RS): sl1, knit to last 2 sts, ssk, turn
Next row (WS): sl1, purl to last 2 sts, p2tog, turn
Next row: knit across the (10, 12, **14, 16**) heel sts left

gusset: Change to MC and work as follows:
Round 1: Pick up and knit 7 (10, 10, **12, 16**) sts along edge of heel flap, continue as established in ribbing across the 14 (18, 22, **26, 30**) sts at top of foot, pick up and knit 7 (10, 10, **12, 16**) sts along edge of heel flap, k4 (5, 6, **7, 8**) to centre back of heel: this is the new beginning of the round. [36 (48, 54, **64, 78**) sts]

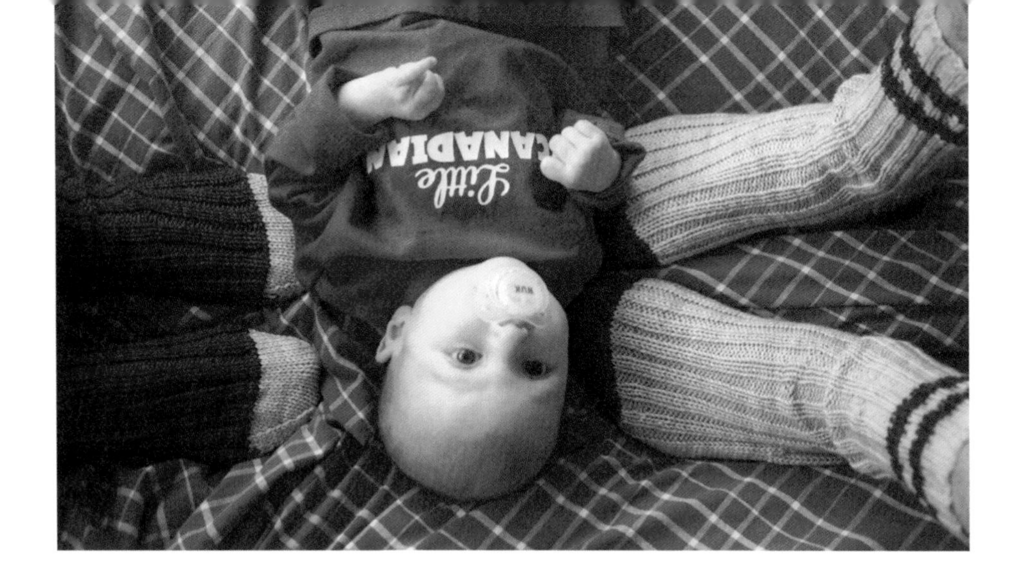

Arrange stitches on 3 double pointed needles as follows: **N1** has 4 (5, 6, **7, 8**) sts from heel, plus 7 (10, 10, **12, 16**) sts picked up from heel flap. **N2** has 14 (18, 22, **26, 30**) sts from the top of the foot. **N3** has 7 (10, 10, **12, 16**) sts picked up from heel flap and 4 (5, 6, **7, 8**) sts from heel.

Round 2: **N1** - knit. **N2** - [p2, k2] three (4, 5, **6, 7**) times, p2. **N3** - knit.
Round 3: **N1** - knit to last 3 sts, k2tog, k1. **N2** - [p2, k2] three (4, 5, **6, 7**) times, p2. **N3** - k1, ssk, knit to end of round. [2 sts dec]

Repeat rounds 2-3 until there are 7 (9, 11, **13, 15**) sts on **N1**, 14 (18, 22, **26, 30**) sts on **N2**, and 7 (9, 11, **13, 15**) sts on **N3**. [28 (36, 44, **52, 60**) sts total]

For the foot, continue as established in pattern *(ribbing across the top of the foot and stockinette stitch across the bottom).*

Baby (Toddler, Child): work 10 (26, 32) rounds.
Mama (Papa): work until foot is 1.75" (2.25") short of desired length.

All sizes: knit to the end of **N1**. The beginning of the round will be at the start of **N2** for the toe.

toe: Change to CC, and work as follows:

Round 1: knit
Round 2: **N2** - k1, ssk, knit to last 3 sts, k2tog, k1. **N3** - k1, ssk, knit to end of needle. **N1** - knit to last 3 sts, k2tog, k1. [4 sts dec]

Repeat rounds 1-2 until 16 (20, 24, **28, 28**) sts remain, then repeat round 2 until 12 (16, 16, **20, 20**) sts remain. Slip sts from **N3** and **N1** onto one needle, graft the toe closed using **Kitchener stitch**, and weave in ends.

H
9
NEUN

waffles

simple and yummy stroller blankie ❤ *by Alexa Ludeman*

There is nothing better than home-made waffles on a Sunday morning! This blanket captures the fluffy waffle texture, knits up quickly, and will keep your wee one warm in the stroller. Pattern includes instructions for chunky and aran weight yarns.

sizing:

Blanket measures approximately 25" wide x 28" long

Note: This is a stroller sized blanket. For a wider blanket, increase the number of cast on stitches by a multiple of three.

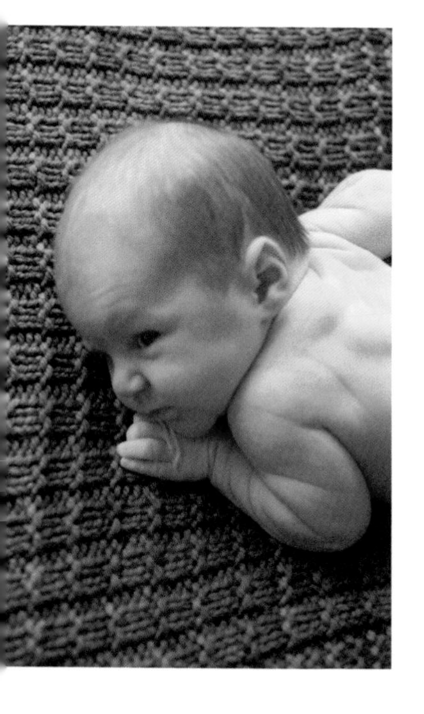

materials:

Yarn: 360 yds of chunky or 600 yds aran weight yarn
(we used ***Madelinetosh Tosh Vintage*** *in 'copper penny' and* ***Dream in Color Groovy*** *in 'grey tabby')*

Needles: Chunky version: US # 10.5 / 6.5 mm
Aran version: US # 9 / 5.5 mm *(or as req'd to meet gauge);*
circular needle 24" or longer

Gauge: Chunky version: 12 sts / 4" in stockinette stitch
Aran version: 17 sts / 4" in stockinette stitch

pattern: *instructions are given for chunky (aran) versions*

Cast on 71 (102) sts. Knit 10 (16) rows.

Row 1 (RS): k8 (10), p1, [k2, p1] to last 8 (10) sts, k8 (10)
Row 2 (WS): k9 (11), [p2, k1] to last 11 (13) sts, p2, k9 (11)
Row 3: k8 (10), p1, [k2, p1] to last 8 (10) sts, k8 (10)
Row 4: knit

Repeat rows 1-4 until piece is approximately 26" long. Knit 10 (16) rows. Bind off loosely and weave in ends. Bundle up baby and get strollin'!

tic tac toe

punk rock baby chic ❤ *by Alexa Ludeman*

Alexa and I are children of the 80's. The defining style moments of our formative years involved slouch socks, bodysuits, and neon. These legwarmers are a nod to our own childhood favorites - Rock on BABY!!

sizing:

To Fit: Baby (Toddler, Child, Adult)

Baby: 5" unstretched, 10" stretched around / 6" long
Toddler: 6" unstretched, 12" stretched around / 9" long
Child: 7" unstretched, 14" stretched around / 12" long
Adult: 8" unstretched, 16" stretched around / 16" long

To adjust length simply add or subtract pattern repeats.
One pattern repeat (rounds 1-24 of pattern) = 2" of length

materials:

Yarn: 150 (250, 350, 550) yds of sock weight yarn
*(we used **Madelinetosh Tosh Sock** in 'poprocks' and **Indigo Moon Merino Superwash** in 'moss')*

Needles: US #2 / 2.75mm *(or as required to meet gauge);* double pointed or circular needles

Gauge: 28 sts / 4" in stockinette stitch

Notions: cable needle, darning needle

tic tac toe cable chart

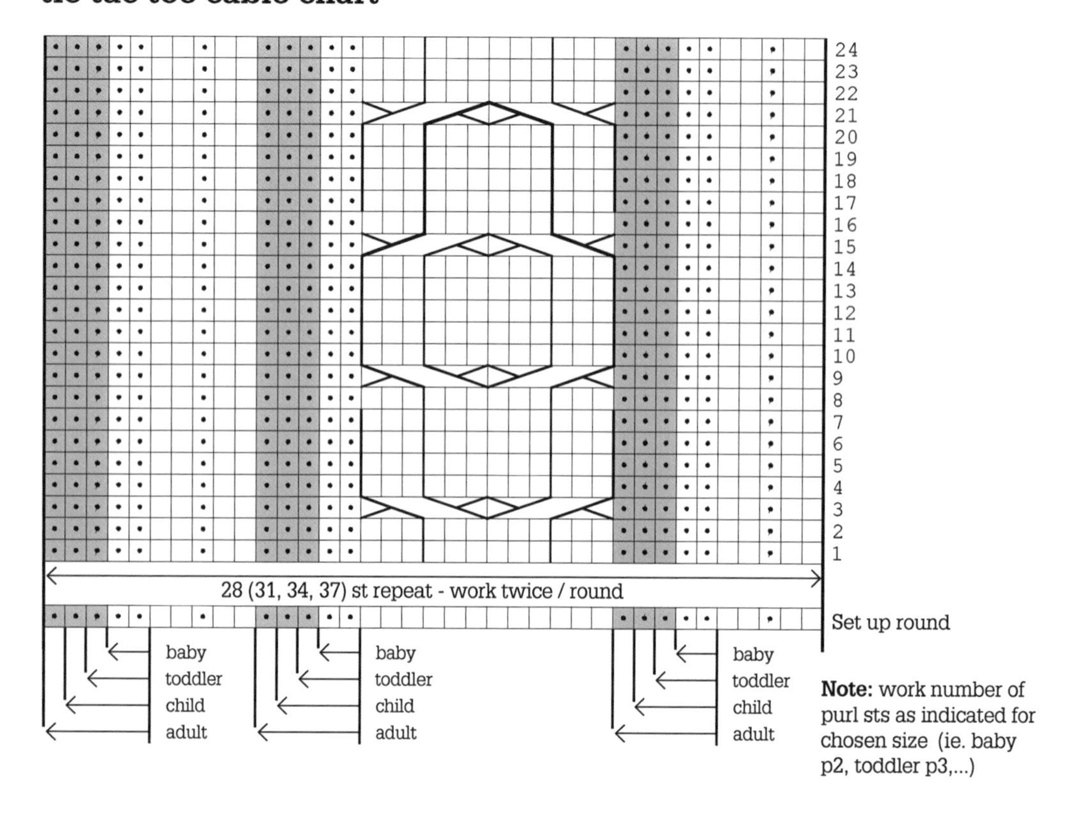

Note: work number of purl sts as indicated for chosen size (ie. baby p2, toddler p3,...)

key & abbreviations

- **k** - knit
- **p** - purl
- **c6b** - cable 6 back - slip 3 sts to cn, hold in back of work, k3 from LH needle, k3 from cn
- **c6f** - cable 6 front - slip 3 sts to cn, hold in front of work, k3 from LH needle, k3 from cn
- shade indicates stitch to be worked on some sizes, but not others

pattern:

Cast on 56 (62, 68, 74) sts loosely, and join for working in the round.

Ribbing: [k1, p1] around

Repeat this round a total of 8 (12, 16, 16) times.

Set up round: [k2, p1, k2, p2 (3, 4, 5), k12, p2 (3, 4, 5), k2, p1, k2, p2 (3, 4, 5)] twice

To work cabled section of legwarmers, repeat the instructions below, or follow tic tac toe cable chart. Pattern is a 24 round repeat.

Rounds 1, 5, 7, 11, 13, 17, 19, 23, and all even rounds (2, 4, 6...):
work as set up round

Rounds 3 & 9: [k2, pt1, k2, p2 (3, 4, 5), c6b, c6f, p2 (3, 4, 5), k2, p1, k2, p2 (3, 4, 5)] twice

Rounds 15 & 21: [k2, p1, k2, p2 (3, 4, 5), c6f, c6b, p2 (3, 4, 5), k2, p1, k2, p2 (3, 4, 5)] twice

Work rounds 1-24 a total of 2 (3, 4, 6) times.

Ribbing: [k1, p1] around

Repeat this round a total of 8 (12, 16, 16) times. Bind off loosely in pattern. Knit second legwarmer, put on Duran Duran, and rock out!

branching out

simple and geometrical lace shawl ❤ by Emily Wessel

Inspired by the fractal geometry of tree branches, this lace pattern increases in complexity and detail as the shawl grows in size. Knit in gourmet fibres this lightweight luxury makes breastfeeding in public as stylish and comfortable as possible!

sizing:

Shawl measures approximately 60" across and 26" in length, (68" x 30" for large size) depending upon gauge, yarn and needle choices, and how aggressively you block the finished piece.

materials:

Yarn: 600 (850) yds lace weight yarn
*(we used **SweetGeorgia Merino Silk Lace** in 'cypress', and **Plymouth Ecco Cashmere** in 'natural / undyed')*

Needles: US #5 / 3.75mm *(or as required to meet gauge);*
24"+ circular needles

Gauge: 26 sts / 4" in stockinette stitch

Notions: stitch markers, waste yarn, crochet hook, darning needle, blocking wires *(if desired)*

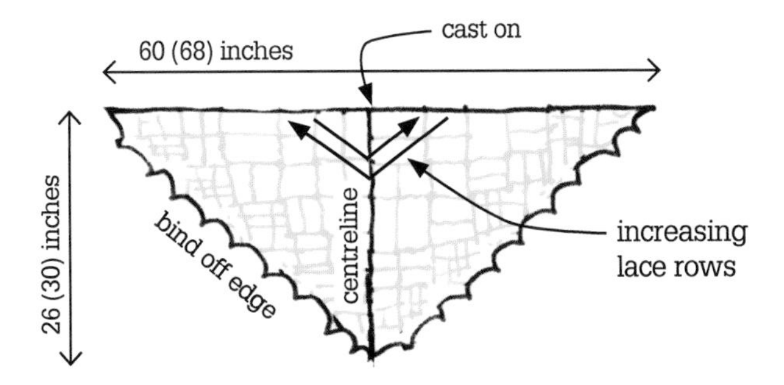

pattern: This triangular shawl is knit in one piece from the centre back point to the edging, and is formed of 2 triangles separated by a centre back stitch which creates a vertical line between the two triangles which make up the shawl. As you will notice, this shawl is asymmetrical.

garter tab cast-on: Cast on 3 sts provisionally. Knit 6 rows. Knit 7th row, then pick up 3 sts along the border of the small garter stitch rectangle you have knit, then undo provisional cast on, put the 3 cast on sts on a needle, and knit them. [9 sts total]. *OR, if you prefer, simply cast-on 9 stitches using any method desired.* Next, work the first wrong-side row: k3, p3, k3, and proceed to chart A: setup.

lace body of shawl: For charts A to F, read rows from right to left, working the 3 edge stitches, the body of the chart, the centreline stitch, then repeating the body of the chart again (from right to left), and finishing with 3 edge stitches.

All wrong-side (even numbered) rows throughout shawl are worked as follows: k3, purl to last 3 sts, k3.

It is useful to place a marker before the centreline stitch as a reminder. You may also use stitch markers to indicate each stitch repeat.

Work rows 1-48 of chart A : set up one time	[105 sts]
Work rows 1-32 of chart B : transition 1 one time	[169 sts]
Work rows 1-16 of chart C : medium lace 1 (2) time(s)	[201 (233) sts]
Work rows 1-16 of chart D : transition 2 one time	[233 (265) sts]
Work rows 1-8 of chart E : small lace 2 (3) times	[265 (313) sts]
Work rows 1-4 of chart F : tiny lace 5 times	[305 (353) sts]

edging: The edging chart G is not split by the centreline stitch. Work the 3 edge sts, then work the main body of the chart over all 'shawl body' stitches [299 (347) sts] and end with the 3 edge sts.

Work rows 1-14 of Chart G : edging one time	[317 (365) sts]

bind off: Bind off all stitches using a stretchy bind off method. One that works well is: k1, [k1, place both sts back on LH needle, and k2tog-tbl] repeat to end. Cut yarn and pull through final stitch.

finishing: Weave in ends, wet block your shawl, and enjoy.

chart A : set up - work rows 1-48 one time

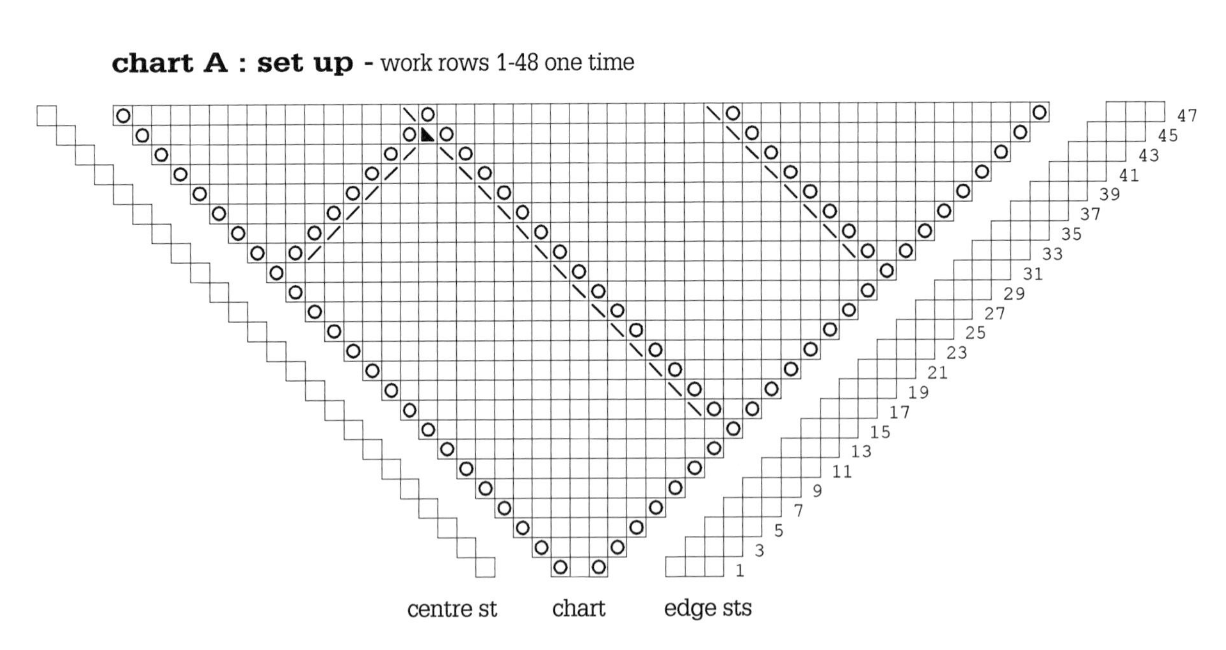

chart B : transition 1 - work rows 1-32 one time

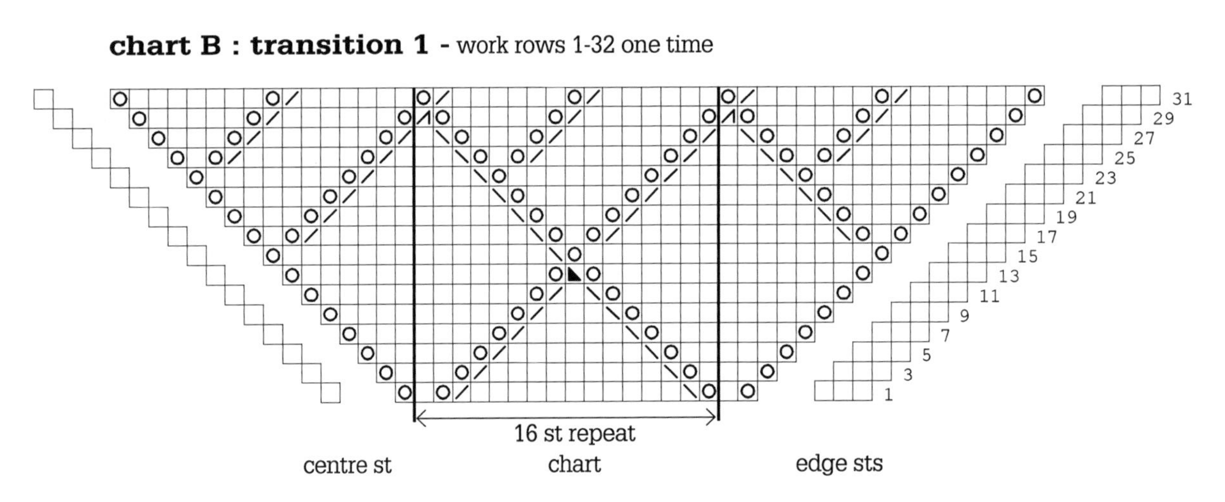

chart C : medium lace - work rows 1-16 one (two) time(s)

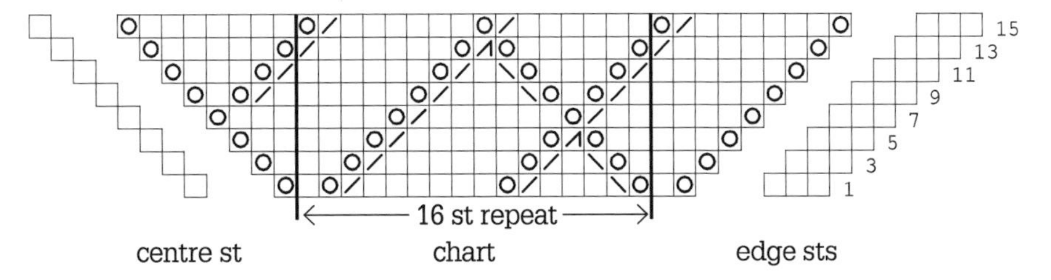

chart D : transition 2 - work rows 1-16 one time

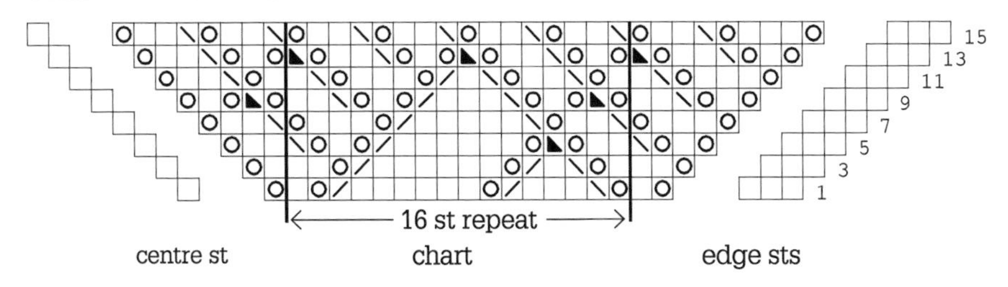

chart E : small lace - work rows 1-8 two (three) times

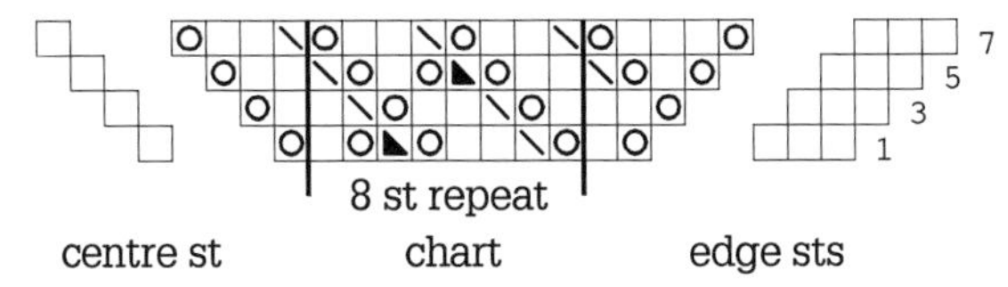

chart F : tiny lace - work rows 1-4 five times

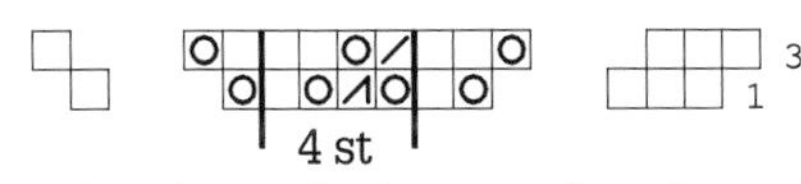

key & abbreviations

- **k** - knit
- **yo** - yarn over
- **k2tog** - knit 2 together
- **ssk** - slip, slip, knit - slip 1 knitwise, slip 1 knitwise, knit 2 slipped sts together tbl
- **k3tog** - knit 3 together
- **sl1-k2tog-psso** - slip 1, k2tog, pass slipped st over

chart G : edging - work rows 1-14 one time * *note: this chart is worked across centreline st* *

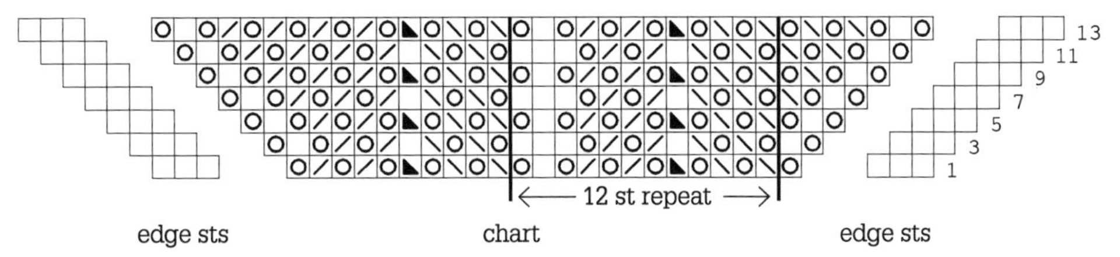

hunter

pine scent and pom poms ❤ *by Alexa Ludeman*

Babies are always cute in cables and pompoms, and this hat makes good use of both. The pattern includes sizes for the whole family so don't stop at just one! Hunter, the hat's namesake, loves to be dressed in fashionable little knits while wandering the forests of British Columbia with her Dad.

sizing:

To Fit: Newborn (Baby, Child, Adult)
Head circumference: 13 (15, 17, 20) inches

materials:

Yarn: 100 (150, 175, 200) yds of worsted / aran weight yarn
*(we used **Madelinetosh Vintage** in 'grove' and 'fig', and **SweetGeorgia Superwash Worsted** in 'ginger' and 'cayenne')*

Needles: US #8 / 5.0mm *(or as required to meet gauge)*;
DPNs and 16" circular needle

Gauge: 18 sts / 4" in stockinette stitch

Notions: cable needle, darning needle

chart A - newborn and child sizes

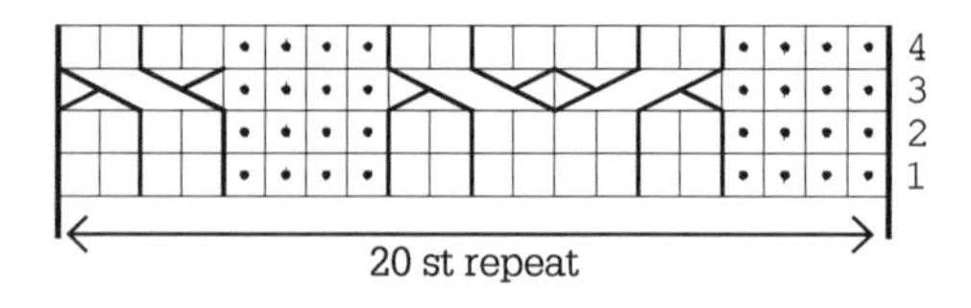

chart B - baby and adult sizes

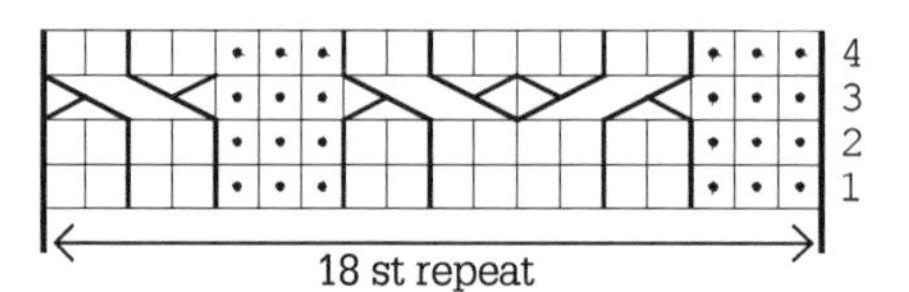

key & abbreviations

- **k** - knit
- **p** - purl
- **c4b** - cable 4 back - slip 2 sts to cn, hold in back of work, k2 from LH needle, k2 from cn
- **c4f** - cable 4 front - slip 2 sts to cn, hold in front of work, k2 from LH needle, k2 from cn

pattern:

Hunter is knit in the round from brim to crown. Follow instructions and refer to charts for chosen size.

newborn size (child size):

Cast on 60 (80) sts. Place marker and join for working in the round.

Ribbing: [k1, p1-tbl] around
Work 9 (11) more rounds in ribbing as established.
Knit 1 round.

Cable pattern: *(also see chart A)*
Rounds 1, 2, 4: [p4, k8, p4, k4] around
Round 3: [p4, c4b, c4f, p4, c4f] around

Work rounds 1-4 a total of 5 (11) times, then work rounds 1-3 once more. Decrease as follows:

Round 5: [p1, p2tog, p1, k8, p1, p2tog, p1, k4] around [54 (72) sts]
Round 6: [p3, k8, p3, k4) around
Round 7: [p2tog, p1, k8, p2tog, p1, k4] around [48 (64) sts]
Round 8: [p2, c4b, c4f, p2, c4f] around
Round 9: [p2tog, k8, p2tog, k4] around [42 (56) sts]
Round 10: [p1, k8, p1, k4) around
Round 11: [p1, k8, p1, ssk, k2tog] around [36 (48) sts]
Round 12: [p1, c4b, c4f, p1, c2f] around
Round 13: [p1, ssk, k4, k2tog, p1, k2] around [30 (40) sts]
Round 14: [p1, k6, p1, k2] around
Round 15: [p1, k1, ssk, k2tog, k1, p1, k2] around [24 (32) sts]
Round 16: [p1, c2b, c2f, p1, c2b] around
Round 17: [p1, k2tog, ssk, p1, ssk] around [15 (20) sts]
Round 18: [p1, k2tog, p1, k1] around [12 (16) sts]
Round 19: [k2tog] around [6 (8) sts]

baby size (adult size):

Cast on 72 (90) sts. Place marker and join for working in the round.

Ribbing: [k1, p1-tbl] around
Work 11 (13) more rnds in ribbing as established.
Knit 1 round.

Cable pattern: *(also see chart B)*
Rounds 1, 2, 4: [p3, k8, p3, k4] around
Round 3: [p3, c4b, c4f, p3, c4f] around

Work rounds 1-4 a total of 8 (13) times, then work round 1 once more. Decrease as follows:

Round 5: [p2tog, p1, k8, p2tog, p1, k4] around [64 (80) sts]
Round 6: [p2, c4b, c4f, p2, c4f] around
Round 7: [p2tog, k8, p2tog, k4] around [56 (70) sts]
Round 8: [p1, k8, p1, k4) around
Round 9: [p1, k8, p1, ssk, k2tog] around [48 (60) sts]
Round 10: [p1, c4b, c4f, p1, c2f] around
Round 11: [p1, ssk, k4, k2tog, p1, k2] around [40 (50) sts]
Round 12: [p1, k6, p1, k2] around
Round 13: [p1, k1, ssk, k2tog, k1, p1, k2] around [32 (40) sts]
Round 14: [p1, c2b, c2f, p1, c2f] around
Round 15: [p1, k2tog, ssk, p1, ssk] around [20 (25) sts]
Round 16: [p1, k2tog, p1, k1] around [16 (20) sts]
Round 17: [k2tog] around [8 (10) sts]

finishing (all sizes): Draw yarn through remaining stitches and pull tight to close top of hat. Make pompom, and attach firmly to hat, and weave in all ends. Toddle to your heart's content!

gramps

stylish outerwear for your grouchy little old man

❤ *by Emily Wessel and Alexa Ludeman*

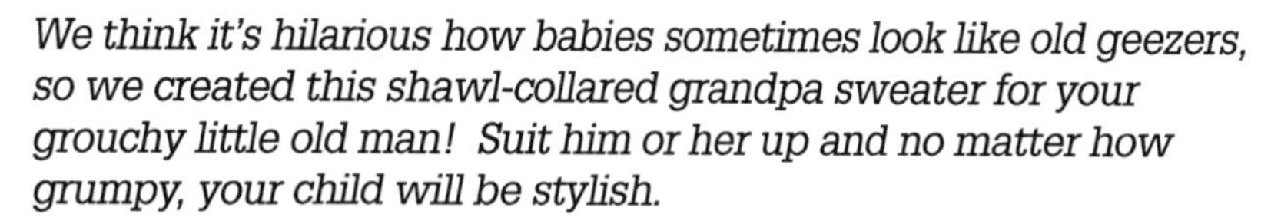

We think it's hilarious how babies sometimes look like old geezers, so we created this shawl-collared grandpa sweater for your grouchy little old man! Suit him or her up and no matter how grumpy, your child will be stylish.

And YES, despite reasonable common-sense notions, babies DO require pockets to store their tiny little pipes, and patches to prevent them from wearing holes through the elbows of their cardigans after years of use! You can make an adorable matching sweater for yourself too.

materials:

Yarn: Worsted / Aran weight yarn - see table following page for yardage *(we used **Madelinetosh Vintage**. Hunter is wearing size 2-4 in 'robin red breast' and 'whiskey barrel', Jones is wearing 6-12 mo in 'whiskey barrel' and 'well water', and Emily is wearing size S in 'smoke' and 'charcoal')*

Needles: US #7 / 4.5mm and US #6 / 4.0 mm *(or as req'd to meet gauge);*
baby - 6-8 yrs: 32"+ circular and DPNs in each size
8-10 yrs - Ladies L: 40"+ circular and DPNs in each size
Ladies XL - 4XL: 47"+ circular and DPNs in each size, plus 16" circular in larger size for upper sleeve

Gauge: 20 sts and 28 rows / 4" in stockinette *(on larger needles)*

Notions: 5 (5, 5, 5, 5, 7, 7, 7, **7, 7, 7, 9, 9, 9, 9, 9, 9**) 1/2" buttons, stitch markers, darning needle

sizing:

Pattern includes 8 child and 9 adult sizes. While adult sizes are named based on typical ladies sizes, this design is completely unisex - for a man simply choose a size based upon the finished measurements desired.

Note: Finished garment measurements given; choose size based on your measurements + desired ease. Gramps is intended to be worn with 1" positive ease at chest. Sleeve and body lengths are easily adjusted.

Size	Chest	Sleeve	Hem to Underarm	Upper Arm	Yardage MC / CC
0-6 mo	20"	6"	6"	7"	240 / 110
6-12 mo	22"	6.5"	6.5"	7.5"	260 / 140
1-2 yrs	23"	7"	7"	8"	320 / 180
2-4 yrs	24"	8"	8"	8.5"	420 / 200
4-6 yrs	25.5"	10"	10"	9"	480 / 200
6-8 yrs	27"	12"	12"	9.5"	460 / 220
8-10 yrs	28.5"	14"	14"	10"	650/ 250
10-12 yrs	30"	16"	14"	10.5"	650 / 300
Ladies XS	**33"**	**18"**	**15"**	**11"**	**750 / 350**
S	**35.5"**	**19"**	**16"**	**12"**	**850 / 350**
M	**38"**	**19"**	**17"**	**13"**	**900 / 375**
ML	**42.5"**	**20"**	**18"**	**14"**	**1100/ 400**
L	**44"**	**20"**	**18.5"**	**14.5"**	**1200 / 425**
XL	**49"**	**20"**	**19"**	**15.5"**	**1500 / 425**
XXL	**52"**	**21"**	**19"**	**17"**	**1600 / 450**
3XL	**56"**	**21"**	**20"**	**18"**	**1700 / 450**
4XL	**59.5"**	**21"**	**20"**	**19"**	**1800 / 475**

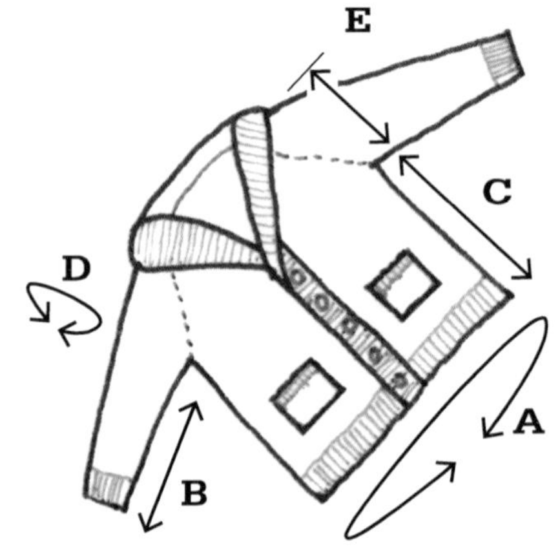

A - chest / bust
B - sleeve
C - hem to underarm
D - upper arm
E - yoke depth (given in pattern text)

pattern:

The jacket is a seamless design, knit from the neck down. After the body and arms are complete, the button band and collar are worked. Pockets and elbow patches are added last. Sweater body is worked in stockinette stitch.

yoke:

Using larger needles and MC, cast on 31 (33, 33, 35, 35, 41, 43, 45, **53, 55, 63, 69, 65, 67, 69, 73, 79**) sts.

Set up row (WS): purl 2 (2, 2, 2, 2, 2, 2, 2, **4, 4, 4, 5, 5, 5, 6, 6, 6**) sts *(right front)*, PM, purl 4 (4, 4, 4, 4, 6, 6, 6, **6, 6, 8, 8, 6, 4, 4, 4, 4**) sts *(right sleeve)*, PM, purl 19 (21, 21, 23, 23, 25, 27, 29, **33, 35, 39, 43, 43, 49, 49, 53, 59**) sts *(back)*, PM, purl 4 (4, 4, 4, 4, 6, 6, 6, **6, 6, 8, 8, 6, 4, 4, 4, 4**) sts *(left sleeve)*, PM, purl 2 (2, 2, 2, 2, 2, 2, 2, **4, 4, 4, 5, 5, 5, 6, 6, 6**) sts *(left front)*

Row 1 (RS): [knit to 1 st before marker, m1, k2, m1] 4 times, knit to end [8 sts inc]
Row 2 and 4 (WS): purl
Row 3: k1, m1, [knit to 1 st before marker, m1, k2, m1] 4 times, knit to last st, m1, k1 [10 sts inc]

Work rows 1-4 a total of 6 (7, 7, 8, 8, 9, 9, 10, **10, 11, 12, 13, 13, 16, 15, 17, 20**) times. [139 (159, 159, 179, 179, 203, 205, 225, **233, 253, 279, 303, 299, 355, 339, 379, 439**) sts]

Work rows 1-2 two (1, 2, 1, 1, 0, 1, 0, **1, 1, 0, 1, 3, 0 5, 4, 0**) more time(s). [155 (167, 175, 187, 187, 203, 213, 225, **241, 261, 279, 311, 323, 355, 379, 411, 439**) sts total; 22 (24, 25, 27, 27, 29, 30, 32, **35, 38, 40, 45, 47, 53, 51, 57, 66**) sts at each front, 32 (34, 36, 38, 38, 42, 44, 46, **48, 52, 56, 62, 64, 68, 74, 80, 84**) sts at each sleeve, 47 (51, 53, 57, 57, 61, 65, 69, **75, 81, 87, 97, 101, 113, 119, 129, 139**) sts at back]

Place locking stitch markers or safety pins in the fabric at the beginning and end of this row.

Work 6 (6, 6, 8, 10, 12, 12, 12, **12, 12, 14, 14, 14, 10, 4, 0, 0**) more rows in stockinette stitch, or until yoke depth measures approximately 5 (5, 5.5, 6, 6.5, 7, 7, 7.5, **7.5, 8, 9, 10, 10, 10.5, 10.5, 11, 11.5**) inches from cast on, ending with a WS row.

separate sleeves and body:

Removing markers as you go, knit to marker *(left front)*, place next 32 (34, 36, 38, 38, 42, 44, 46, **48, 52, 56, 62, 64, 68, 74, 80, 84**) sts on hold *(left sleeve)*, CO 4 (4, 4, 4, 6, 6, 6, 6, **8, 8, 8, 8, 8, 10, 10, 10, 10**) sts using backward loop method *(left underarm)*, knit 47 (51, 53, 57, 57, 61, 65, 69, **75, 81, 87, 97, 101, 113, 119, 129, 139**) sts *(back)*, place next 32 (34, 36, 38, 38, 42, 44, 46, **48, 52, 56, 62, 64, 68, 74, 80, 84**) sts on hold *(right sleeve)*, CO 4 (4, 4, 4, 6, 6, 6, 6, **8, 8, 8, 8, 8, 10, 10, 10, 10**) sts using backward loop method *(right underarm)*, knit to end *(right front)*.

[99 (107, 111, 119, 123, 131, 135, 145, **161, 173, 183, 203, 211, 239, 251, 271, 291**) body sts]

You will now work back and forth in rows to complete the body with sleeve stitches on hold.

body:

Work in stockinette stitch until body measures 5 (5.5, 5.5, 6.5, 8.5, 10.5, 12.5, 12.5, **13, 14, 15, 16, 16.5, 17, 17, 18, 18**) inches from underarm, *(or 1 (1, 1.5, 1.5, 1.5, 1.5, 1.5, 1.5,* ***2, 2, 2, 2, 2, 2, 2, 2, 2****) inches short of desired length)*, ending with a purl row.

Change to smaller needles and CC and knit 1 row.

Ribbing:
Row 1 (WS): p2, (k1, p1), to last 3 sts, k1, p2
Row 2 (RS): k2, (p1, k1), to last 3 sts, p1, k2
Work rows 1-2 until ribbing measures 1 (1, 1.5, 1.5, 1.5, 1.5, 1.5, 1.5, **2, 2, 2, 2, 2, 2, 2, 2, 2**) inches. Bind off all stitches loosely in pattern.

sleeves: *(work each the same)*

Place 32 (34, 36, 38, 38, 42, 44, 46, **48, 52, 56, 62, 64, 68, 74, 80, 84**) held sts on larger DPNs *(or 16" circular needle for larger sizes)*. Knit across these sts, then pick up and knit 2 (2, 2, 2, 3, 3, 3, 3, **4, 4, 4, 4, 4, 5, 5, 5, 5**) sts from underarm, PM, pick up and knit 2 (2, 2, 2, 3, 3, 3, 3, **4, 4, 4, 4, 4, 5, 5, 5, 5**) more sts. Knit around to marker, this is the new beginning of round, located at underarm.
[36 (38, 40, 42, 44, 48, 50, 52, **56, 60, 64, 70, 72, 78, 84, 90, 94**) sts]

Knitting every round work for 1 (1, 1, 2, 3, 3, 4, 6, **6, 6, 6, 5, 5, 5, 4, 3, 3**) inches. *Note: if you are altering the sleeve length, this is a good place to do it.*

Decrease round: k1, k2tog, knit to last 3 sts, ssk, k1
Knit 5 rounds.

Repeat the previous 6 rounds 2 (3, 3, 4, 4, 6, 6, 6, **8, 9, 10, 13, 12, 13, 15, 17, 17**) more times, until 30 (30, 32, 32, 34, 34, 36, 38, **38, 40, 42, 42, 46, 50, 52, 54, 58**) sts remain.

Work in stockinette stitch until sleeve measures 5 (5.5, 5.5, 6.5, 8.5, 10.5, 12.5, 14.5, **16, 17, 17, 18, 18, 18, 19, 19, 19**) inches *(or 1 (1, 1.5, 1.5, 1.5, 1.5, 1.5, 1.5,* ***2, 2, 2, 2, 2, 2, 2, 2, 2****) inches short of desired length).*

Change to smaller needles and CC and knit 1 round. Work in 1x1 rib (k1, p1) for 1 (1, 1.5, 1.5, 1.5, 1.5, 1.5, 1.5, **2, 2, 2, 2, 2, 2, 2, 2, 2**) inches. Bind off all stitches loosely in pattern.

button band and shawl collar:

The button band and shawl collar are worked at once, markers separate the work into five sections. Use CC and smaller circular needle.

Right front: With RS facing, starting at the bottom of right front, pick up and knit approximately 3 sts in every 4 rows to locking stitch marker, ending with an **even number of sts** in this section. Remove locking marker and place a marker on the needle,

Right neckline: continue, picking up and knitting approximately 1 stitch in every row to cast-on, ending with an **odd number of sts** in this section, then PM,

Back neck: continue, picking up and knitting one stitch in each cast on stitch, PM,

Left neckline: continue, picking up the same number of sts as right neckline to next locking marker. Remove locking marker and place marker on needle,

Left front: continue, picking up the same number of sts as right front to bottom of left front.

After picking up, there should be an **odd number of sts** to each side of the back neck section.

Set up (WS): p1, [k1, p1] to second marker, kfb to 1 st before next marker, k1, [p1, k1] to last stitch, p1

Ribbing (RS): k1, [p1, k1] to end

For the remainder of collar, continue ribbing as established (knit the knits, and purl the purls).

short row collar shaping:

Setup row A (RS): Work in ribbing to 2 (2, 2, 2, 2, 2, 2, 2, **4, 4, 4, 4, 4, 4, 4, 4, 4**) sts past fourth marker, w&t
Setup row B (WS): Work in ribbing to 2 (2, 2, 2, 2, 2, 2, 2, **4, 4, 4, 4, 4, 4, 4, 4, 4**) sts fourth marker, w&t

Short row 1 (RS): Work to 3 (3, 3, 3, 3, 3, 3, 3, **4, 4, 4, 4, 4, 4, 4, 4, 4**) sts before the gap, w&t
Short row 2 (WS): Work to 3 (3, 3, 3, 3, 3, 3, 3, **4, 4, 4, 4, 4, 4, 4, 4, 4**) sts before the gap, w&t

Work short rows 1-2 a total of 3 (4, 5, 6, 7, 8, 10, 11, **12, 12, 14, 14, 15, 15, 16, 16, 16**) times.

Next 2 Rows (RS, WS): Work in ribbing to end of row, picking up wraps and working them together with the stitches they wrap.

Adult sizes only: work 2 more rows in ribbing.

Work buttonhole row (RS): Work 5 (5, 5, 5, 5, 7, 7, 7, **7, 7, 7, 9, 9, 9, 9, 9, 9**) buttonholes *(described below)*, evenly spaced before first marker, then work in pattern to end.

Note: for a manly sweater place buttonholes on left front, evenly spaced between the fourth marker and end of row.

To make a 3-st buttonhole in 1 row: Slip next 2 sts. Pass the first st over the second (bind off), [sl 1, bind stitch off] twice. Slip stitch from RH needle to LH needle. Turn work and CO 3 sts knitwise. Turn back and proceed to work to next buttonhole.

If you find this buttonhole is too big or too small, you can work similar buttonholes by binding off then casting on 1, 2, or 4 sts in the same manner.

Work 3 (3, 3, 3, 3, 3, 5, 5, **5, 5, 5, 5, 5, 5, 5, 5, 5**) more rows in pattern.

bind off: On a RS row, bind off in pattern to second marker, then continue binding off at back neck using a decreasing bind-off as follows: [k2tog, pass first stitch over second and off needles], repeat to next marker, then bind off remaining sts in pattern.

pockets: *(work 2 the same)*

Using larger needles and MC, starting 5 (5, 5, 5, 5, 7, 7, 7, **9, 9, 9, 9, 11, 11, 11, 11, 11**) rows above ribbing and 5 (5, 5, 5, 5, 7, 7, 7, **9, 9, 9, 9, 11, 11, 11, 11, 11**) sts from button band, pick up and knit 11 (15, 17, 17, 19, 19, 23, 23, **23, 23, 25, 25, 25, 27, 27, 27, 27**) sts with RS facing.

Beginning with a purl row, work 11 (15, 17, 17, 19, 19, 23, 23, **23, 23, 25, 25, 25, 27, 27, 27, 27**) rows in stockinette, then change to smaller needles and CC and knit 1 row.

Row 1 (WS): p2, [k1, p1] to last st, p1
Row 2 (RS): k2, [p1, k1] to last st, p1

Work rows 1-2 a total of 2 (2, 2, 2, 2, 2, 2, 2, **3, 3, 3, 3, 3, 3, 3, 3, 3**) times, then work row 1 once more. Bind off all sts in pattern, then sew sides of pocket down.

elbow patches: *(work 2 the same)*

Using smaller needles and CC cast on 9 (9, 9, 9, 11, 11, 11, 11, **13, 13, 13, 13, 15, 15, 15, 15, 15**) sts.

Row 1 (RS): purl
Row 2 (WS): k1, m1, k to last st, m1, k1
Repeat rows 1-2 until there are 13 (13, 13, 13, 15, 15, 15, 15, **19, 19, 19, 19, 21, 21, 21, 21, 21**) sts.

Work 3 (3, 3, 3, 5, 5, 5, 5, **9, 9, 9, 9, 11, 11, 11, 11, 11**) rows even in stockinette.

Row 3 (WS): k1, ssk, knit to last 3 sts, k2tog, k1
Row 4 (RS): purl
Repeat rows 3-4 until there 9 (9, 9, 9, 11, 11, 11, 11, **13, 13, 13, 13, 15, 15, 15, 15, 15**) sts, then bind off.

finishing:

Weave in ends and block sweater. Sew buttons in place to align with buttonholes. Sew patches to elbows of sweater, purl side facing out.

Stuff your kid (or yourself!) into this sweater and venture out to grouch around the playground. Grin and appreciate the fruits of your labour because it is certain that your child will not!

gone fishin'

undersea mobile or knitted toys for baby's room ❤ *by Alexa Ludeman*

This colourful collection of undersea creatures can be made into a mobile to hang above the crib, or simply used as toys which are sure to delight your little one.

sizing:

Big Fishy: 10.5" around, 8.5" long (including tail)
Little Fishy: 10" around, 6.5" long (including tail)
Octopus: 10.5" around, 10" tall (including legs)
Starfish: 5.5" across
Seaweed: 8" (12") long

materials:

Yarn: worsted / aran weight yarn (in several colours)

Big Fishy: 90 yds MC, 20 yds CC
Little Fishy: 65 yds MC, 20 yds CC
Octopus: 120 yds MC
Seaweed: 20 yds MC
Starfish: 80 yds MC
(we used ***Malabrigo Worsted*** *in 'natural', 'lettuce', and 'jewel blue')*

Needles: US #6 / 4.0 mm *(or as required to meet gauge)*; DPNs and 20"+ circular needle

Gauge: 20 sts / 4" in stockinette stitch

Notions: stitch markers, waste yarn, darning needle, polyfill, floral wire (for octopus), buttons, dowelling, and fishing line

**** Note: Buttons or safety eyes can be a choking hazard for infants, and floral wire can also be dangerous. If an infant will be left unsupervised with toys or mobile, use embroidered eyes instead, and omit floral wire.*

big fishy, little fishy: Fishy is knit from lips to tail, then fins are added. Both fishies follow same pattern, with slight differences as noted.

lips: Using i-cord cast-on and CC, cast on 12 sts. Distribute these 12 sts over 3 double pointed needles (4 sts per needle). [k2tog] around [6 sts]. Cut CC, leaving an 8" tail.

body: Change to MC, knit one round. Setup for increases: [k1, PM] around. You will have 6 markers *(preferably an odd coloured one to indicate the start of the round)* and one stitch between each marker.

Round 1:	[knit to marker, m1, slip marker] around	[6 sts inc]
Rounds 2-3:	knit	

Big Fishy: Work rounds 1-3 a total of 8 times until there are 54 sts.
Little Fishy: Work rounds 1-2 a total of 8 times until there are 54 sts.

Stop knitting at this point to weave in ends and use the CC tail to draw up lips and sew up the gap in the i-cord cast on.

Round 4:	[knit to 2 sts before marker, k2tog] around	[6 sts dec]
Rounds 5-6:	knit	

Big Fishy: Work rounds 4-6 a total of 6 times, then round 4 once more.
Little Fishy: Work rounds 4-5 a total of 6 times, then round 4 once more.

There will now be 12 sts. Stop knitting and stuff your fishy. If using safety eyes, attach them now.

tail: To close the body and begin the tail, slip the first 6 sts onto needle 1 and the last 6 sts onto needle 2 (removing markers). Then slip all 12 sts onto 1 needle, alternating between needles 1 and 2 (slipping one stitch from needle 1, then one from needle 2). Now all stitches are on a single needle. Change to CC and shape tail as follows.

Row 1:	kfb, knit to end	[1 st inc]

Repeat row 1 until there are 24 sts. Knit 1 more row, then bind off.

fins: *(make two the same)*
Using CC pick up 12 sts along the side of the fish (as shown in photos). *Alternately, you can cast on 12 sts, knit the fins separately, then sew them to the side of your fishy.*

Row 1:	knit	
Row 2:	k2tog, knit to last 2 sts, ssk	[2 sts dec]

Repeat rows 1-2 until 2 stitches remain.

Next row: sl1, k1, pass slipped stitch over. Cut yarn and pull tail through the last loop. Weave in all ends and sew on buttons, patches or embroider eyes.

octopus: Octopus is knit from the legs up to the top of the head.

legs: Make 8 legs of 3 stitch i-cord, each 6" long, leaving the last 3 stitches of each i-cord live. Distribute these 24 sts over three DPNs.

head:

Round 1: [k2tog] around [12 sts]
Round 2: [k2tog] around [6 sts]
Round 3: [k2tog] around [3 sts]
Round 4: [kfb] around [6 sts]
Round 5: Set up for increases: [k1, PM] around
You will have 6 markers *(preferably an odd coloured one to indicate the start of the round)* and one stitch between each marker.

Round 6: [knit to marker, m1, slip marker] around [6 sts inc]
Round 7: knit

Work rounds 6-7 a total of 10 times until there are 66 sts. Knit 2 rounds even.

Round 8: knit
Round 9: [knit to 2 sts before marker, k2tog] around [6 sts dec]

Work rounds 8-9 a total of 6 times until there are 30 sts. Stop knitting and stuff your octopus. If using safety eyes, attach them now. Work rounds 8-9 two more times [18 sts]. Work round 9 once more [12 sts].

Cut yarn, leaving a 5" tail. Add final bit of stuffing, then thread tail through remaining live stitches and secure. Weave in ends and sew on eyes. For an octopus with stiffer and more curly legs insert floral wire; but do not use floral wire if octopus is to be used as a toy.

seaweed: Instructions are for small (large) sizes.

Using circular needle cast on 24 (36) sts.

Round 1:	knit	
Round 2:	[kfb] across	[48 (72) sts]
Round 3:	knit	
Round 4:	[kfb] across	[96 (144) sts]
Round 5:	knit	

Bind off and weave in ends.

starfish:

body (make 2): Cast on 10 sts using **pinhole cast-on method**. Distribute stitches on DPNs.

Round 1:	knit	
Round 2:	[m1R, k1, m1L, k1] around	[20 sts]
Round 3:	knit	
Round 4:	[m1R, k1, m1L, k3] around	[30 sts]
Round 5:	purl	
Round 6:	knit	
Round 7:	[m1R, k1, m1L, k5] around	[40 sts]
Round 8:	knit	
Round 9:	[m1R, k1, m1L, k7] around	[50 sts]
Round 10:	purl	

Place sts on waste yarn 10 sts at a time. You will have 5 pieces of waste yarn with 10 sts on each. Cut yarn.

After knitting second body piece (same as the first), leave yarn attached, and place the first 10 stitches on one needle. Place the remaining 40 sts on waste yarn 10 sts at a time.

arms: *(repeat 5 times to form each of the 5 arms)*

Take 10 sts from the first body piece, and 10 sts from the second body piece and distribute these 20 sts over 3-4 DPNs. You will proceed to knit in the round to form one of the five arms.

Rounds 1-3:	knit	
Round 4:	[k2tog, k2] around	[15 sts]
Round 5:	purl	
Rounds 6-8:	knit	
Round 9:	[k2tog, k1] around	[10 sts]
Round 10:	purl	
Rounds 11-13:	knit	
Round 12:	[k2tog] around	[5 sts]

Cut yarn, leaving a 6" tail. Weave tail through remaining live stitches and secure. Repeat for remaining 4 arms. Once you have completed all 5 arms, you can stuff the starfish through the gaps between the arms. Lastly, use yarn ends to sew up these gaps, then weave in ends.

mobile construction:

Materials: 2 pieces of dowelling each approximately 12" long. Yarn or fishing line and 8 buttons (optional).

Note: The sea creatures hanging from opposite ends of the same piece of dowelling should be similar in weight. These instructions are for eight sea creatures, if you have more we suggest adding them in multiples of two so that you can still have a similar weight distribution.

step 1: Drill 2 holes into each end of the dowelling; the first approximately 0.5" from the end, and the second 1" away from the first. This will accommodate 8 sea creatures (4 on each piece of dowelling).

step 2: Using yarn lash together the 2 pieces of dowelling so they form a cross.

step 3: Using fishing line (or yarn) attach sea creatures to the holes in the dowelling. There are a couple of different ways to do this:

Either Cut a double length of fishing line and attach it to the sea creature by threading it through. Attach the other ends of the fishing line to the mobile by threading one end through the hole and tying the two ends together.

Or Cut a double length of fishing line, attach one end of the fishing line to the sea creature by threading it through. Attach one end through the hole in the dowelling. Then thread each end of the fishing line through a button and knot it.

step 4: Cut 4 lengths of yarn or fishing line, about 2.5 feet in length. Tie the yarn around the dowelling between the two sea creatures, repeat for the other 3 sides. Tie the other end of these 4 lengths together in a knot.

step 5: Attach another length of yarn or fishing line to the knot you just tied, and use this line to hang the completed mobile from a hook in the ceiling.

dogwood

fresh and lacy baby blanket ❤ *by Emily Wessel*

This darling baby blanket adds a sweet and romantic touch to any room. The bold graphic is as fresh as the spring and the new life that it brings.

sizing:

Finished blanket will measure from 36 to 40 inches square; depending on gauge, yarn, and how aggressively you block the squares.

materials:

Yarn: 750 yds of worsted / aran weight yarn
*(we used **Dream in Color Classy** in 'beach fog')*

Needles: US # 8 / 5.0 mm *(or as required to meet gauge)*; DPNs and / or circular needles as desired for knitting in the round

Gauge: 18 sts / 4" in stockinette stitch

Notions: stitch markers, darning needle, 4.5 - 5.5 mm crochet hook, blocking wires *(if desired)*

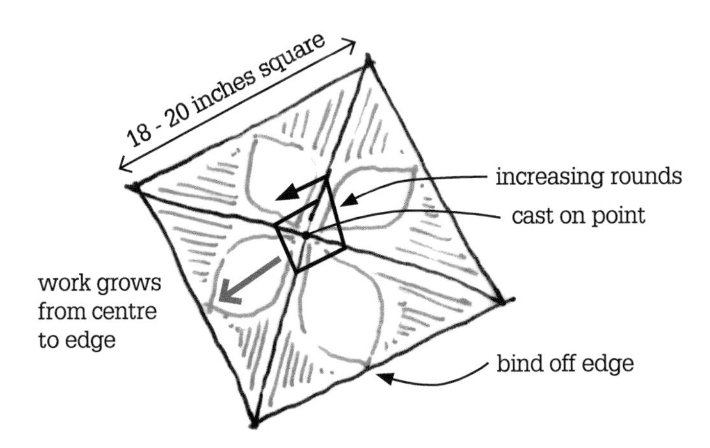

pattern: Each square is knit in the round, from the centre outward.

Cast on 8 stitches using the **pinhole cast-on method**. Work the following set-up rounds *(also shown on dogwood square chart)*:

Round 1: [k1, yo] around [16 sts]
Round 2 and all other even rounds: work as established; knit the knits and yarn-over sts, purl the purls and p3tog sts from the previous round
Round 3: [k1, yo, k3, yo] around [24 sts]
Round 5: [k1, yo, k1, yo, sl1-k2tog-psso, yo, k1, yo] around [32 sts]
Round 7: [k1, yo, k1, ssk, yo, k1, yo, k2tog, k1, yo] around [40 sts]
Round 9: [k1, yo, k1, ssk, yo, k3, yo, k2tog, k1, yo, m1] around [52 sts]

Work rounds 11-54 following dogwood square chart. Chart is repeated four times each round. Each odd numbered round adds 8 sts to the total stitch count. On all even rounds, work as established *(purl the purls and p3togs from previous round, knit all other sts)*. After round 54, there will be 228 sts.

dogwood square chart

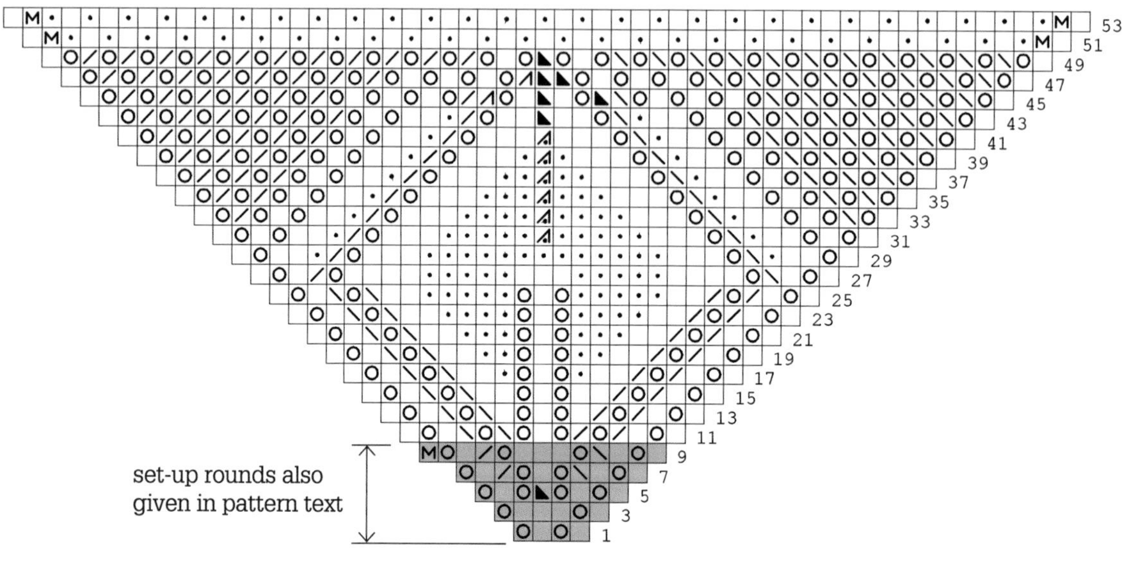

bind off: If you are a loose knitter, a standard bind off works well for this project. If you are a tighter knitter, you could use the following stretchy bind off: k1, [k1, place both stitches back on LH needle, and k2tog-tbl], repeat to end. After binding off the first square, block it immediately to determine whether the bind off method used allows the square to be blocked to the desired size. If not, use the stretchy bind-off noted above.

finishing: After completing four squares, block each to the same dimensions (18" - 20" square). Holding wrong sides together, sew squares together using a **slip stitch crochet seam** (or mattress stitch). The edges will stand up and form a ridge on the right side of the blanket. Weave in ends and block the blanket again if desired.

key and abbreviations

- ☐ **k** - knit
- ⊡ **p** - purl
- O **yo** - yarn over
- M **m1** - make 1
- ⁄ **k2tog** - knit 2 together
- \ **ssk** - slip, slip, knit - slip 1 knitwise, slip 1 knitwise, knit 2 slipped sts together tbl
- **k3tog** - knit 3 together
- **sl1-k2tog-psso** - slip 1, knit 2 together, pass slipped stitch over
- **p3tog** - purl 3 together

chart notes: Chart is read from right to left and from round 1 to 54. Only odd number rounds are shown. All even number rounds: work as established - purl the purls and p3tog sts from the previous round, knit all other sts.

thank-yous

we ❤ you all so much

Many people have participated in our journey from concept to finished book - thank you so much! It has been a pleasure to knit with you.

Most especially we would like to send hearts and rainbows out to:

- The knitters who support us by purchasing our patterns and recommending our work to others; you are the reason we can continue to create and publish designs!
- Our families and friends for their love and support.
- Our models for contributing their time and good looks.
- Our test knitters and tech editors for their hard work, diligence and helpful suggestions.
- **www.ravelry.com** for providing a fabulous online community for knitters and independent designers.
- All the fabulous local yarn stores who support and promote our work.

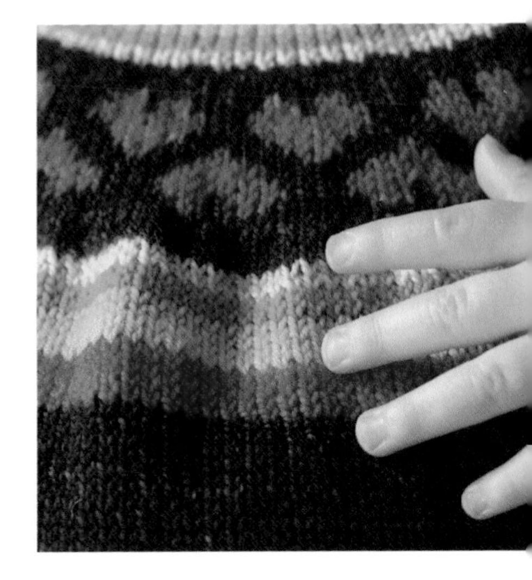

Love our work? Sign up for our email updates to hear about the latest designs, tutorials, and subscriber specials!
www.tincanknits.com/contact

other Tin Can Knits designs you'll love :::

low tide

vivid

antler

pop blanket

lush

stovetop

CPSIA information can be obtained
at www.ICGtesting.com
Printed in the USA
LVIC04n1337201215
467103LV00007B/25